D1050814

EXCUSED ABSENCE
FORM

VIRGINIA
TRUDI

TRUDI!!

Feel free to color this page

The Mostly True Stories of Trudi Hierholzer

ISBN 978-0-57-868745-2 (paperback)
ISBN 978-0-57-868746-9 (ebook)

✳ ✳ ✳

BOOK DESIGN: Leslie Saunderlin, lesliesaunderlin.com

GRAPHIC DESIGNER: Jeremiah Lewis

ILLUSTRATOR: Meam Hartshorn

EDITORS: Anne Westrick and Shelia Shedd, swiftcreative.net

ACKNOWLEDGEMENTS

Trudi Hierholzer – Thank you Mom & Dad for the vast life
experiences. It's been interesting.
Jon Rakestraw – Thanks to Meam Hartshorn for the illustrations
and Professor Read Baldwin and Robin Ball for facilitating.
Gratitude goes out to Anne Westrick, my editor, who brought
order to this work. Thanks to my family for their support.

TABLE OF CONTENTS

In Hot Water

Dealing With Bullies

Dodged That Bullet

IN HOT WATER

Snake

Ever since I was little, my mom's nickname for me was "Snake." She called me Snake cuz she said I was mean as a snake. My grandma and grandfather owned some property with a farm in Disputana, Virginia, and also woods around it. All of us used to go walking in the woods all the time. Mama told me she used to have me walk ahead of everybody because there wasn't an animal in the woods meaner than me. Not only was I a tough girl, but she told me that I've been running my own life since I was six. So pretty much since six I have been taking care of me.

I have three sisters. My dad had a daughter from his first marriage. Later, my dad married my mom. They had three children and I am the middle of those three. My oldest sister is nine years older than I am. The next oldest is two and a half years older than I am and my baby sister is 15 months to the day younger than I am.

Back then I couldn't stand my youngest baby sister, Robbi. She was a tattletale and my mother made me take her everywhere. She said I was old enough to babysit or something. She was only a year and three months behind! I guess my reputation as the mean mature "Snake" was mom's reasoning. Ah, what a pain it was to have her tag along!

The worst pain was, after returning home from our adventures, Robbi would tell mom her version of the day. Well, you might have guessed, it was always much worse than what had really happened. Such as one time when I got in super serious trouble thanks to her. My cousins Lisa and Shari were over visiting. They were sisters. Lisa is one

month older than me and Shari is a year and a half younger than me. So, the four of us were hanging around and I was made to take them with me when I left the house. Ugh. So I took them with me. About halfway up the block, we ran into an old friend of mine nicknamed "Cricket." She was at least 3 years older than I was and very pretty. Her nickname was Cricket on account of the boys saying that's the sound her legs made when they were rubbing together. She was a smoker. I didn't smoke. She usually would ask me if I wanted to smoke while she was sitting there talking to some guy. They were smoking and so she offered a cigarette. And I'd say, "No, I'm not interested." I kept saying no every time we met.

So, the day when I showed up with my cousins and sister, Cricket did not bother asking me. But she did ask Robbi and my two cousins if they would like to try smoking. Surprisingly, they said yes. I didn't. They had a way out, because I replied, "No." They could've said no without looking terrible. I had already said no, but no, they all tried smoking!

When we got back home, my mom probably smelled it on us. I don't remember who fibbed but it was likely my tattle-tale sister. Because they smoked, I got in trouble. Go figure! I didn't smoke, right? Despite me pleading to mom that I had refrained, mom said, "You're in trouble because it is your friend and you put them in a bad situation."

Ugh!!! My friend! Cricket was really my friend's friend. Not a true friend, but that didn't matter to mom. She said, "You oughta have known better than to take them that way."

"Wha!?" I said. "She's not really a friend of mine, and you're the one that made me take them!"

Well, my reasoning did not sit well with mom. I got in trouble because it was my friend. I didn't smoke!!!

Now, do I sound like a snake to you?

Comparing Notes

One day, I really didn't feel like going to school....
There was no special reason; I just didn't want to
deal with it. So I wrote up an excuse, forging my dad's
name. The next day I went to the front office at Colonial
Heights High School to show my excused absence.

The nurse, Mrs. Story, read my note, looked at me, and
said, "This note is a fake." I said, "No it's not! My dad
signed it." I pointed to the signature.

She got up and went to my file. She pulled out a thick
folder; I had missed a lot of days. She compared the note

with the others. Amazingly, she could not tell the difference. I was good and still am. If you need a forgery, let me know, but it'll cost ya!

Still not convinced, the nurse called Vice Principal Goulder and asked him to take a look at it. He complied. I went to his office, handed him the note, then sat down.

Mr. Goulder studied the note then said, "So, Miss Trudi, forging a note?"

"Nope," I stated.

"Well, let's call your dad and just see if that's the case."

"Fine," I smiled. My dad never answered his work phone. He was very seldom in the office. His office was more like a warehouse. He was always out in the field fixing biomedical equipment, so I was home free.

But, to my surprise, he answered. Still, I figured my dad would surmise I was forging and go along with my escape plan.

Boy was I wrong! My dad told the principal he didn't write a note.

Ugh! I'm in hot water now, I thought to myself.

Mr. Goulder slammed the phone down and said,

"I gotcha! That'll be three days in-school suspension

for you, young lady."

When I finally got home, dad said, "Got caught didn't ya?"

"Why did you answer the phone!?" I asked.

"Why wouldn't I?" he asked back.

"Why couldn't you have said different? I can't believe you

didn't tell him you wrote the note."

I blamed my dad for botching it up. After all, it was his

fault, right? I mean, he should've figured out what I was

doing. Then again, if I were in his shoes, maybe I would've

done the same thing. Ah, I should've just stayed at school.

TRUDI!!!

That's A Lie

One day at high school, my younger sister Robbi had to stay after to make up a history test. I was about to take off with my friend when I decided to check if she needed a ride home.

I popped my head into Ms. Robertson's class and saw Robbi there with a couple of other students. The teacher was just about to hand out the tests.

I said to Robbi, "Do you need a—"

"Excuse me!?" said Ms. Robertson.

"Hi," I said, "I'm just asking—"

"Get out!" boomed Ms. Robertson. "Can't you see I am trying to give out a test? You're being rude."

Wow, I can't believe a teacher is shouting at me, I thought. I matched her tone of voice. "No, I'm not! You haven't started yet."

"Get out means get out!"

Whoa, what a temper, how does she keep her job?

I lowered my voice, "I was just asking my sister if she needed a ride. Robbi, do you need a ride?"

Robbi replied, "Yes, I need one, thanks."

"Okay, I'll be out front. Ms. Robertson, I'm leaving now."

"Good, now get out and shut the door," she said.

"Okay," I replied, "but remember, you asked for it."

Looking back now, I feel bad about what I did next. I was so peeved with the way Ms. Roberston spoke to me, I lashed out. Umm, let's say it was more like I slammed it out....

I grabbed the door and swung it shut with a force that shook all the lockers clear down to the next room.

The door's glass rattled so much it almost shattered.

When I got to the parking lot, my friend was waiting in my VW convertible. She was laughing because she said she could hear that door way out here!

So I was riding the wheel well when I looked back and saw Ms. Robertson staring at me. The next thing I heard was the parking lot PA. "Trudi Hierholzer, please come to the office."

I figured, why should I? School's over. They have no power over me. Then I heard it again. I ignored it. By the sixth time I was just flat out annoyed, so I went to the office.

Once there, I told Vice Principal Goulder my story.

Then, sure enough, here comes Ms. Robertson.

Mr. Goulder states, "Now, Trudi, please let Ms. Robertson tell her side."

Ms. Robertson says, "This young lady would not come down to the office with me."

"That's a lie!" I exclaimed.

"Trudi!" said Mr. Goulder with a penetrating stare.

"She interrupted my class while students were taking the

test," said Ms. Robertson.

"That's a lie! She hadn't started testing yet."

"Trudi, wait your turn," he said.

"Why should I? She's obviously lying," I countered. "I just wanted to ask my sister something. How can she get away with lying right to your face? I didn't do that. 'I tried to get her to come to the office with me' is a bold-faced—"

"Sit down!" Mr. Goulder ordered.

I sat down and said, "I don't have a problem with coming after school to see you Goulder, but—"

"Shut it! And that's Mr. Goulder to you, young lady."

Hmm, should've said "Mr." to help my cause, I thought.

Ms. Robertson went on. Four lies altogether. I interrupted after each lie. Now, I admit, maybe I shut the door a little too hard, but I was just following orders. She was literally yelling at me to get out and I hadn't done anything; she was still holding the tests. How hard was it for her to just wait a few seconds to let me ask my sister something?

If anybody interrupted her class, she did with her stopping

me mid-sentence. It was a quick answer to a quick question. Besides, I didn't know her, and she didn't know me.

So anyway, after she finished her story, Mr. Goulder said, "Okay, so what do you want to do? How would you like me to punish her? Right now, she has no demerits. If you give her five demerits, then she'll have in-school suspension. Give her three and that would leave her hanging on the edge. So whatever you want to do."

She goes, "Give her three."

I said, "That's because she's lying."

"Trudi, that's enough or I'll up it to five," Mr. Goulder said.

Ms. Robertson could have put me in an in-school suspension. But she made a point of making sure that I didn't go to suspension for what I'd done. She knew I was right. I did all the things she asked me to do. I left her class and closed the door, sort of. A couple demerits, what's that?

What would you have done to me?

DEALING WITH BULLIES

Trudi Pootie

So back in 4th grade, there was a young man that was picking on me. His name was Turner. We had some really weird names in our neighborhood. Anyways, his name was Turner and he was always teasing me. He was calling me names. He didn't touch me, but he was still super annoying. He made me mad with names like Trudi Fruitie, Trudi Pootie, Trudi Cootie, and Trudi Bootie. Trudi pretty much rhymes with everything horrible. Oh, it was terrible!

One day after school, he was on a roll with Trudi Bazzutie and Trudi's Got a Big Bootie. So I had had enough and I told him to quit it. But he didn't. Despite the fact that he was in 6th grade and a bit taller than me, I warned him I was gonna knock him out. Although I didn't wanna touch him, because he was constantly picking his nose then eating his boogers or smearing them on the inside of his sleeve. Gross!!!

So I hit him. I don't remember hitting him a lot. But I'm pretty sure Turner cried from the very first punch, so it didn't matter how much I hit him because he was a big cry-baby. The funny thing was, every time I landed a blow my hand hit a bone. I was fighting a skeleton; the kid had no muscle, no fat! After I gave Turner a black eye and a bloody nose, he ran home to tell his mom.

The trouble was his mom was my dad's secretary so she knew how to reach me. She called my mom to tell her Turner just got beat up by me. Now, I don't remember what my Mom said at the time; I was outside pouring salt on a slug. But later on, she was talking to somebody and she goes, "Do you know that Turner's mom called me to tell me that my daughter beat up her son?"

Now, if I had a son, I wouldn't tell anybody that some girl beat him up. So I kept thinking, I wonder if mom told that woman, "Don't go around telling people some girl beat up your son. What's the matter with you?"

The bottom line was I didn't get punished for beating up a bully.

Well, by the next day the word had gotten out, including to the other tough girl in the neighborhood. She was an eighth grader. Her name was Kathy. She was a bit of a tomboy with freckles and pig tails and arms like a boy and a jaw-bone like a big bad bulldog. She definitely had a reputation. You would be wise not to mess with Kathy. She was great, and l loved how she'd crack her knuckles three times—once on her left and twice on her right before spitting on the ground then walloping you in the face. Me being in the fourth grade, she was considerably taller, faster, and way stronger than me. She was so tough, not even a high school football jock would mess with her. Thank God we never really had any dealings with each other until that day. Turner didn't get any satisfaction from the phone call to my mother, so he contracted out his revenge to Kathy. Apparently, my mom gave his mom the impression I was not going to get punished. So after school, Kathy sauntered up to the school grounds and stood in my face to confront me about picking on Turner. Turner was cowering behind her. He was not friends with her. They wouldn't have been friends because there was so much of an age difference, but they were friendly, probably cuz she lived real close to him. Kathy lived two blocks away from me.

Anyways, he knew her really well. I guess he told her that some girl was picking on him at school and asked if she could tell her to stop it. Maybe he also asked if she could do the knuckle thing then beat up the bully.

So she came to the school. I was just leaving because the older kids get out sooner than the younger kids. Anyhow, there Kathy was. She looked mean. She stared at me with furrowed brows, pig tailed fiery red hair, large nostrils flexing in and out with each breath, freckles as big as dimes, and her lower jaw protruding out. She was ready to make a kill. Her feet were in a warrior stance shoulder width apart. She occupied the school playground like she owned it. She was the only thing standing between me and my way home.

Kathy said, "I heard you've been picking on Turner. Well, stop it, or I'll knock you into next week!"

"Seriously," I replied, "Turner was calling me names and he started it."

"Whaaa'?!" Kathy gasped.

"Yep," I said, "all I did was try an' shut him up. And I'm going to tell you this, Kathy. If he calls me another name, I'm gonna hit him again."

She spun around, looking down on him nose-to-nose.

"Hey Turner, you didn't tell me you were calling her names."

Turner looked like he had just seen a ghost. He was seek-

ing words that didn't come. His mouth was shaped as if he were bobbing for apples.

Kathy said, "I'm not gonna get involved if you started it. I thought someone at school had messed with you. I'm not a bully."

So he accomplished nothing. It did not work out for him. He turned and ran back home, crying the whole way.

As for me, I don't start fights. I just finished them. And there was many a time that I had to do such a thing on account of being called Trudi Pootie, Trudi Cootie—blah, blah, you get the point.

Besides Kathy, there were a handful of other so-called tough kids I had to deal with. Unlike Kathy, they were bullies. Most of the time these kids were at elementary school. Sometimes they picked on me, but most of them they teased my younger sister, Robbi. But over time, you go to school with the same people your whole life. They know you. So, by the time I moved onto middle school, I never had to fight again period, for me or for my sister, because

I had a reputation.

From then on, all I had to do was step in and people would step out. So I came to the school to say something to the Somebody about messing with my sister. I didn't want to because that was me being the aggressor. That's not what I'm about. But I didn't mind, because I'm very confrontational. It just didn't bother me. But if I stepped up to say something to the Somebody he or she would say, "Oh, I didn't know she was your sister. Really, we don't have to fight. It's not that big of a deal."

I didn't want to fight. Each time I didn't have to fight, I managed to accomplish what I set out to do without throwing any fists. That worked out for me. Just like that!

Hmm, now that I think about it, I'm glad no one ever made fun of my last name. They could've said, "Hier Holzer, come Hier girl, that's a good dog."

Yeah, I had and have limits, I confess. If someone had used the "that's a good dog" line even up into high school, I'd a walloped them into next week with two black eyes!!!

A Very Long Stick

Okay, so when I was in fourth grade, I was on my way home from school one day and when I got to the sidewalk some kids were running back past me. They said this kid was threatening them up ahead. So I went across the street from the school grounds and there's this little boy with a very long stick. He was just swinging it back and forth and stood in the way of anybody trying to walk down the sidewalk. So I was a little confused about why anybody would be intimidated by this little kid.

So all I did was wait until he swung at me, then walked right up on him. I grabbed the stick and yanked it out of his hands. Then I waved it at him and he took off running. Well, the kids who passed me had gone to the principal and told him about the stick swinger. When the principal came out with these kids to address it, I was the one they found with the stick.

With his hands on his hips, he said, "Trudi, you need to go to the office with me."

I said, "I'm not gonna go to the principal's office. I didn't do anything wrong."

Then he said, "Well, we'll sort this out in the office."

I replied, "Look, it wasn't me. It was a boy and he's running down the street. You can see him there on the other side of the block."

He said, "Well, we'll just straighten it out in the office."

I stated, "I'm not going to the office with nobody."

Then I turned from him and walked home. I lived about six blocks away. Well, this principal knew where I lived

because his niece lived in the house behind us. He started walking behind me. I guess he thought that was going to intimidate me, I don't know. Would you have been intimidated? As he continued walking behind me, I was thinking, "I don't care. You can follow me home."

Anyway, I was almost home and I could see my mom on the porch and she just stood there talking to the neighbor who was also waiting for her child to get home from school. As they were talking across the street from each other, my mom looked over and saw I was almost home. We lived on a corner and I was almost at the opposite corner. Then she noticed the principal behind me about a half a block. And she said, "What did you do now, Trudi?"

I answered, "I didn't do anything. I told him I didn't do anything. Some little boy was threatening other kids with a stick. He was swinging it to hit kids and all I did was take it from him. Then the principal came out, saw me with this very long stick and didn't want to listen. He wanted me to go to the office and I wasn't willing to go."

Well, about that time the principal had made it to our corner where my mom and I were talking. He went to say something and my mom said, "Don't even bother. My daughter is a lot of things, but she's not a liar. She's not the one who did it. If she said she didn't do it, she didn't do it." He was speechless. He had to walk all the way back to school with no one to punish.

What was the principal trying to prove? Was this about his pride because I turned and walked away? Did he want to verify my story with what the other kids had witnessed? Ok, if it was to verify, I got that, but he should have done that the next day. After all, school was out.

Fire Ants

For the most part, my family lived in Colonial Heights, Virginia. But when I entered fifth grade, my dad had to go out of state for job training. He was a repairman fixing medical equipment in the hospital. The training course was going to take ten months. He had to learn how to repair new equipment coming to the hospital. My mom wouldn't let him go all that time by himself. She insisted we go too. So, we ended up in Aurora, Colorado, and it was totally different than what I was used to. We got into the school system and I scoped out the neighborhood. I learned

34

who were the tough kids and who were the wimps.

Now, if you've ever had to switch schools, then you know you've got to figure this out fast. You ask yourself questions like:

- Where am I in the pecking order?
- Who can I push around (if they start messing with me)?
- Who should I avoid?

There's always someone who just wants to mess with you, just so they can prove they're above you. Well, my problem was that if anybody messed with me, I didn't back down. Usually, new kids get beat up, only I didn't get beat up. I was tall for a fifth grader, and mean. Most girls my age would leave me alone. But one day after school, an eighth grade girl chose to pick on me. She pushed me. I pushed her back, and a lot harder at that. I won the fight. After that, some eighth graders took me under their wing. I guess I fit in with them.

Later, we were on the playground and a little boy named Zack was carrying this little clear case which had a bunch of fire ants in it. He was wearing khaki short overalls with an oversized white collared shirt on. He gazed google-eyed at these ants and chuckled to himself. He walked by me. Then it started to get weirder.

Zack looked at his pets and said, "How's my fiery babies today? Are you ready to make them scream? Ehww, you're looking hungry. Let's go munch on some girls!"

He first shows it to this punny fifth grade girl named Emily. Emily was the sweetest little thing with perfectly groomed hair and clean fingernails, and she was always neatly dressed. She was so neat and tidy. I never saw her pick her nose or fart or put her elbows on the table at lunch. That day, she was wearing a green dress with white polka dots. She sported white stockings and black leather patent shoes. When she moved about, it was like a gazelle bouncing to and fro.

"Hey E-m-i-l-y! Look at my new fire ants," said Zack, shoving them in her face.

"Ahhh!" she screamed and ran away.

Next, he zipped on over to Twanda, Suzanne, and Mary-bow Sandler and said, "Hi, I'm gonna throw fire ants on you."

Of course, they all screamed at once and took off.

Now, I was thinkin' that why they were scared of these stupid ants was beyond me. Of course, I was and still am not scared of anything. I used to catch snakes when I was little. I did not fear anything. I'd catch 'em on my grandmother's farm then grandma would burn them.

So, the Fire Ant Boy came my way.

"Trudi Fruitie, you better scootie cause I'm gonna throw my fire ants on you. They're so hungry. These ants will eat your eyes out," said Zack.

I stood my ground with my hands on my hips till he got within an arm's length of me. Then I smacked the case out of his hand and it fell on the ground. The case opened up and the ants started running all around. Some of them ran up his legs and started biting him. He began crying and doing a jig.

"Ah, now you've got ants in your pants!" I said.

You should've seen this kid. He ran zigzag around the playground, bumping into people. Then he stopped and smacked his legs to try and kill the ants. He did the zigzag smack-the-legs move again and again until he was so delirious, he ran into a teacher sipping on a carton of chocolate milk. Fire Ant Boy hit her so hard, she dropped her carton right on top of his head. Some of the milk oozed down his face and some of it got on his starched white shirt.

"What are you doing?" exclaimed the teacher.

"Trudi broke my ant farm," he said as he boohooed past her toward the principal's office.

Wouldn't you know it, things got worse from there for Ant Boy. I followed after him and witnessed the red and black ant collision. The custodian had just finished mopping up a mess in the hallway. Ant Boy ran right past his slippery floor sign and slid a good ten feet into Mr. Wizler, the 6th grade science teacher, who was holding a black ant farm in a plastic box. He knocked Mr. Wizler forward, making him drop the farm right on Zack's head. Lots of sand, dirt, and ants fell on Zack's face. Some of the ants went into his shirt while the rest of them took off throughout the school. Mr. Wizler was lying on his chest moaning. Zack kept running toward the office, now smacking at black and red ants on his face.

I was laughing so hard, like I had ants in my pants. Luckily, I didn't get in trouble since the principal figured out he was scaring little girls.

The rest of the day, I heard kids throughout the school screaming and whacking ants. It was hilarious!

It took two weeks before my mom got around to finishing my school registration. She brought the paperwork to school instead of having me deliver it. She walked into the office and handed the forms to the principal.

He took one look at my mom and said to her, "Oh, you're Trudi's mom, right?"

"Ah, yes, how did you know?" she replied.

"Well, your daughter was in the office for saving a bunch of fifth graders from the Ant Boy."

"Excuse me?" she said.

"Put it this way," he said, "your daughter stopped ants from going down their pants."

"Ah, I think I've heard enough, I got the gist of it."

She turned and walked away. Funny thing was, he never mentioned that the whole school had an ant infestation for a week. Apparently, the ants stuck around to drink the chocolate milk which Zack had managed to spatter everywhere while he was running down the hallway.

I had only been in school two weeks and already I was on top of the pecking order. I had a reputation as the girl who toppled the Fire Ant Boy. No kid pushed me. I didn't have to avoid anybody. I smiled over the fact that my mother told her friends I wasn't in school but two weeks—not registered, supposed to be an unknown—but the principal already knew her child's name. Looking back, it was nice being on top of the hill!

Sled

There's a really, really tall hill just around the corner from where I grew up. We would block off the street for sledding. It was a wild ride down. The hill was long and steep but flattened out near the bottom and divided. It had two median strips—the first with three large oak trees and the second with three crape myrtles. The oak trees were probably how the road got its name, Royal Oak Avenue. When it snowed, and it didn't snow a lot in Colonial Heights, Virginia, but when it did, we would go to that hill and start a fire in a metal barrel.

The city trucks came down the street and made it safe by scattering dirt instead of salt. Nasty stuff! They left dark brown clumps on the road. We would scoop up the dirt and throw it off to the side, then pack the snow. Next, we got it super slick by pouring water on it. The water would harden overnight into a sheet of ice. God help any driver who did go down it. Anybody who did drive it would cuss us out if they saw us.

So, you guessed it. We went down the hill on Flexible Flyers and Canadian toboggans. Right?—WRONG!

Well, today you'd go down on a Flyer or a snowboard, but back then we didn't have snowboards. Most of the time we were sitting on our butts. We used all kinds of stuff: cardboard, sheets of plastic, trash can lids without handles, and even a T-top roof. Yep, you heard right. Some kid was dumb enough to use his dad's T-top panel to sled down. He did it only once because after that he got paddled. He couldn't sit on his rear for a week!

Anyway, we used all kinds of stuff for slides, but you can't control such makeshift sleds, so most of the time we'd wipe out halfway down, collide into each other...you get the picture. It was entertaining to watch, but painful to crash. Kids ended up with black eyes, bruised forearms, cut fingers, and bloody noses, just to name a few injuries. One kid died. He upended his sled by hitting a bump in the road, which hurled him spread eagle into the first median strip's third oak tree. An imprint of his body in the form of a big X is still visible in that tree. Nah, that didn't happen, but I got you believing it for a moment there. Personally, I didn't run into a tree, but several people did. Fortunately, the ones that did were mostly on inner tubes. They bounced off and were okay. A kid named Reggie used to rule the hill with an extra-large inner tube. No kid could beat him down the hill. He was so big and wide at the waist (if you know what I mean) that his sheer weight and low center of gravity got him going quicker than anyone else. Plus, if you started out first, he ran into you, which sent you flying, or he'd push you over into the shrubbery or onto someone's lawn. He loved to challenge kids to a demolition derby-style race. Losers had to pay with a s'mores. We used the fire in the barrel to make them.

Well, one time my friend Judy and I came up with a plan to dethrone Reggie as the King of the Royal Oak Slope. I came to the slope and Judy said, "I'm sick and tired of Reggie beating everyone. I'd like to give him a Wet Willie as he zips by. Maybe that would throw him off and we'd win?"

(A Wet Willie is sucking your pointing finger then sticking it in someone's ear.)

"Yeah, same here," I replied.

"Yeah, but I'd never reach him," pouted Judy.

"Hmm, how 'bout this?" I said.

"What?" she said.

"If you can't reach him with your hand, maybe you can reach him with something else."

"What are you suggesting?" said Judy.

"Is there a broom in your mom's kitchen?" I asked.

"Well, yeah, but my mom would notice it if I took it.

Oh, but there's one in the garage."

"Cool, so here's what I'm thinkin'. You go get the broom, and while you're gone, I'll challenge Reggie to a race. I'll ask for the usual three second head start. He'll say yes. Then, when we line up, you jump on the tube at the last second with the broom and shove us off," I said.

"Then what?" she asked.

"Well, what da you think? As he goes by us, you whack him with the broom and we'll win," I explained.

"Cool!"

Judy ran off to fetch the broom. When I saw her coming back, I sprang the plan into action.

"Hey, Big Butt!" I shouted.

"Who are you calling Big Butt?" said Reggie.

Reggie had blazing bright red hair and wore a sweater that said, "Bug Off!" He stank. I don't think that kid took a shower. He bullied all the kids in the neighborhood and he'd crack his neck by shifting it from side to side then show his teeth before he'd say something demeaning. The worst was, he always had crud caked around his nostrils. Plus, he'd fart half the time out of that big butt of his. Yeah, you're thinkin' this kid must have been gross. Well, you'd be right. Anyways, back to the story.

"I'll race you! Loser has to pay two s'mores," I said.

"You're ON!" he exclaimed.

"Bet you can't beat me with a three second head start!"

"Are you kiddin'? You're a girl and I'm twice your size. No problem, you're ON! I'm gonna knock you and your tube into next week!"

"Yeah right, I'm gonna put your eyeballs where the sun don't shine!" I countered.

"Okay, let's line up, Trudi Turd face," ordered Reggie.

"Ah, this is gonna be good," snickered Edwin, who was in charge of lining up racers and doing the "1-2-3, go!"

Reggie and I lined up at the top of Royal Oak Avenue. By this time Judy was standing two feet behind and just smiled at me. I smiled back.

Edwin checked that we were lined up right. Then he said, "Okay, Trudi Fruitie, when I say '1-2-3 go,' you take off. Reggie, I'll say '1 Mississippi, 2 Mississippi, 3 Mississippi,' then you go. Got it?"

"Yeah, we got it," I said.

"Yep," said Reggie. We lined up. "You're gonna be eating snow poop as I go by, bird brain!"

"They're gonna scrap your insides off that oak tree," I replied, pointing to one of the three oaks in the median strip.

"Ready," said Edwin, looking at me, "set, 1-2-3-go!"

Just then, Judy jumped on with her broom.

"Hey," said Reggie, "you two are dead!"

Edwin was on "3-Mississippi" when Reggie took off. Because Judy and I had doubled the weight on our tube, it took Big Butt a few seconds to catch up. We swerved to the outside lane and I thought we were goners since Judy had to readjust her broom as Reggie came by on the inside. But it all worked out, 'cause in our swerve we hit a patch of powder and kicked up snow in Reggie's eyes.

He was momentarily blinded. Judy swiveled and aimed the broom for his shoulder but caught him in the face. Some of the icy bristles hit him in the eyelids, others his forehead and still others went up his nose. The nose job got him.

"Ahhhh!" he cried, falling backward off his tube then rolling end over end into the third oak tree.

"We did it!" I said. "Yahoo!" Judy said, laughing her head off as we reached the bottom of the hill.

By the time we got back to the top of Royal Oak Avenue, Reggie was long gone. Edwin ran up and grabbed my and Judy's arms and hoisted them up in front of the other kids and cried, "The winners!"

"Where's Reggie?" I asked.

"Oh, he took off with a black eye and tears running down his face," said Edwin.

We never got our s'mores. It didn't matter. We were the

new kings of Royal Oak Hill and Reggie never

bad-mouthed anyone again. Hmm, now I'm hungry after

telling you this story. Think I'll make some s'mores!

DODGED THAT BULLET

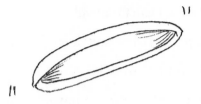

Frisbee

My sister and I were always getting into something. My sister was usually with me because my mother made me take her everywhere I went. We spent a lot of time outside our house, where we would throw a frisbee back and forth. We were good at it. We'd stand across the street from each other and throw it when the cars weren't coming. That kept us pretty occupied for a while. Then we decided it'd be really cool to skip it off the road. Well, soon enough we got pretty good at that too. Our aim was true. We could pop it off the road right into the other person's hands. No cars, of course, until one day.

What day that was, I can't remember. Anyhow, we decided maybe we'd skip the frisbee one time when a car was coming. "It'd be funny," we said.

So, I said, "Okay, for this car coming up, we need to wait and throw it between the front tires and the back tires." Now, it was kind of tricky because drivers did not respect the 25-mph road sign. Since they were not doing 25, it served them right that these two kids would be so bratty. Also, we were very young. If I remember right, we were definitely not in middle school, so we were roughly elementary school age. Anywho, we made up our minds; we were going to throw the frisbee and skip it on the road between the front and back tires.

As people were driving down the street, all kinds of things happened. Sometimes our frisbee hit the road in front of the car, other times beside it or behind it. Sometimes it glided right over top of the car. Lots of times we'd get it just right. The frisbee skipped between the front and back tires, landing right in our hands. What a thrill when we got it right! Oh, but when we got it wrong, we really got it wrong. A bunch of times we couldn't get the frisbee across in time and they would run over it. You'd hear clunk, clunk. Sometimes we'd hit the car's undercarriage and you'd hear a mixture of sounds between a grinding sound and a ker-plunk. No matter what it was, whether it hit the road or it hit the tire or it hit the car, we caused them to stop.

Yep, you can imagine what happened next, but it was slightly worse than that. They stopped the car, got out, and started cussing at us, even though we were just kids! Granted, we were bratty kids, but still. And, you know, let this sink in for a sec. These are adults, not teenage drivers cussing out two little kids. My mom was probably in the house. If not, she was grocery shopping, but most of the time she was in the house and she did not come out.

So, we were on our own with a lunatic driver.

I wish mom did come out the day we had to deal with the YMCA lady. We hit her front tire. She had a fancy car.

She stomped on the brakes, skidding to a halt. She must have been doing at least 35. She jumped out wearing a YMCA track suit. It was a horrid orange color with double white stripes down the sides. She wore a ton of makeup, with fake eyelashes and ruby red lipstick. She looked like an avatar in a video game. Like the others, she started cussing us out. I dare not repeat what she said, since it was really nasty.

Then something came over me, and I responded, "Serves you right! You're speeding down MY street!"

She replied, "What did you say to me?"

"You heard me."

My sister said, "Um, ah, Trudi, maybe we should say we're sorry."

"Shut it," I snapped at my sister.

YMCA ordered, "Where's your mother?"

I answered, "None of your beeswax, Y-M-C-A."

"Now look here, you little brat. Come here right now and take me to your mother," demanded YMCA.

"Not on your life, lady. You're nuts," I said.

Well, then it got really crazy. The YMCA lady lost her noggin. She ran out of the street towards me. My sister stood there dumbfounded.

Can you believe it? YMCA lady left her car running in the middle of the street with the driver door open and hazard lights blazing. She hustled over and tried to grab me, so I took off. I'd figured 'cause she was middle aged, she was not gonna follow me. But the lady followed me. I guess since she goes to the Y, she thought she could catch me. WRONG!

Anyway, I was running down the sidewalk, going past Mr. Simpson. He was blind and he had a seeing eye dog named Herbert to show him the way. Herbert was a really good dog; he always pooped in the grass. But that day, as I was going down the sidewalk, Herbert pooped on the sidewalk. So, I came up with a plan lickety-split since the Y lady was gaining on me.

I ran right over where the poop was, hoping she'd step in it.

Well, what'd ya know, she did get it, and in a big way. She stomped right in the middle of the poop, sliming her ultra-white sneakers. She slid forward, landing kerplunk face first in a puddle of water. Just my luck!!!

"Ahh, that's it," she cried. "It's over for you!"

She recovered with a mixture of water and mud on her tracksuit and a patty of poop stuck to her right foot. She renewed the chase with greater vigor. By this time, I had climbed over Mr. Carlson's metal fence. She followed, but as she was clearing the fence, her left shoelace caught on a barb in the top of the fence. That sent her head first into the grass and her left shoe went flying. Meanwhile, I had stumbled over Mr. Carlson's tree stump and fallen over too. She got excited about my fall, thinking she'd finally catch me. She leaped up, as did I, and the chase resumed. Now she was a shoeless YMCA lady, so she couldn't run as fast.

"Hey, lady, what are you doing?" exclaimed Mr. Carlson.

"Nothin'! This kid damaged my car," replied Y lady. As she was talking, I doubled back and jumped Mr. Carlson's fence again. She did the same.

Looking back, it beats me why I did that. Anyways, she was close on my tail, holding her shoe. Back at the road where it all started, she finally grabbed ahold of me.

"Now you're gonna pay, you little brat. Where's your home?" she demanded.

"Ah, lady, I'm not gonna pay. You are," I answered.

"What are talking about?" she asked.

"Look behind you," I said.

"Wha', hey, wait a minute!" she exclaimed, watching the Dixie Wixie tow truck haul away her car. "Wait! No! That's my car!" she yelled, letting go of me.

"Come back here!" She took off after the truck down the middle of the street. "You can't do that!"

Well, needless to say, I didn't stop, but took off back to the house, and that was the last I ever saw of the YMCA lady.

Coordination Trick

Every summer, my mom was always looking for places to send my sisters and me. She just wanted to get rid of us, I guess. Anything would do. She signed us up for any sport or craft camp. If there was a camp for playing Tiddlywinks, we were going. Most of the time, it was church camps. I wish there had been a Survival Camp for Girls where you'd go into the Shenandoah forest for a week with a canteen, matches, pocket knife, and a slingshot. You'd have to make your own wooden teepee and eat grilled rabbit on a stick. Of course, I'd sneak a bag of cheese curls to go with it. Oh, and a pack of gum to freshen my breath and blow bubbles.

Ho-hum, it was mainly church camps. And it wasn't just our Baptist church camp or another Baptist camp in the area. We would go to every Vacation Bible School for every church in Colonial Heights. As long as they didn't overlap with each other, my mom made it happen.

One time I went with my church group to a camp in Pocahontas Park. The park was designed for kids to stay a week. They had cabins on one side of the campus for boys and the other side for girls. Most of us were fourteen or so, including myself. I attended a traditional Baptist church, so girls had to wear dresses and they couldn't be seen at the same time in the camp pool with boys and stuff like that. However, we did have a dance—go figure. Bottom line is, it was very strict.

But we did compete in sports against boys. The camp gave out trophies. All week long, camp staff had you doing things like archery, rowing, and shooting rifles.

We did baseball games and swimming competitions and mud wrestling. Okay, mud wrestling—I wish! Anyway, it was all kinds of activities, and at the end of the week, staff gave out trophies to those who were the best at all these things. I earned a few trophies.

But by far the most fun we had was playing practical jokes on each other. Usually this was on other girls. There were several churches represented, and each church had their own cabin. It was fun to be around the people you knew, plus you got to intermingle with other girls. Our chaperones were a youth pastor and his wife. She was cool and helped us organize all kinds of games and activities against other cabins.

One time the pastor's wife got us invited for a get together with the cabin next to us. I don't even know what church it was, but they already knew our group were a bunch of pranksters. The night before, we had snuck into their cabin and put their hands in warm water so they wet their beds. We put shaving cream in their hands then tickled their noses with feathers, causing them to slap themselves.

So, the next morning some cabin buddies and I went over to apologize, and we hung out a bit. The real reason we went was to scope the place out to see everybody before the get together. The walls were lined with bunk beds and had an open area in the middle. The kitchen had its own building that included a dining area for everyone to eat together. Bathrooms were in a different place. This kept the smell down.

From our first visit, we learned about the girls' habits, where they all slept, and if there were any booby traps. I noticed they had this bucket full of water inside next to the door. If anybody tried to mess with them, they could throw cold water on you.

We usually picked on the biggest and the meanest girl in the group, and this time was no different. Yeah, call us crazy; we usually were. So, we decided our target for the get-together at two o'clock would be the tallest and meanest girl there. I think her name was Hillary. I don't really remember for sure, but anyway, Hillary was a hill; she was big and tall. She shriveled up her face like a dried prune when she got mad. If you got her really angry, she'd do the shrivel up thing and clench her fists. I imagined that if she went berserk, she would take a whack at you.

Two o'clock came and we went over to their cabin for board games, chitchat, and any other activities we came up with. My buddies started to chat with Hillary. While they were distracted, I moved the bucket under a bunk bed. This way, they couldn't retaliate.

I said to Hillary, "We have this coordination trick I bet you can't do."

She replied, "Yeah, well, we'll see about that."

"Okay," I said, "then sit down here on the floor with your legs apart and take these sticks. One in each hand." She did so. The sticks were six-inch-long branches with a slight point at the ends. Then I poured a cup of water on the floor between her legs.

"Hey, what's the deal?" she said.

"Oh, that's part of the trick," I said as my friend and I held a towel at opposite ends stretched near her ankles. "You're supposed to stab us with these sticks before we can mop up the water. It's a coordination trick. Think you can beat us?"

"No problem," Hillary said. All she was thinking about was the fun she would have stabbing us. She and her friends had forgotten about the bucket.

"Ok," I said, "on three, we start. Got it?"

"Got it."

"All right, ready? On three. One-two-three!"

My friend and I dropped the towel, grabbed a leg, then pulled Hillary through the puddle before she could stab us. Then we let her go and turned for the door. My buddies took off for the woods, but I slipped in the puddle and fell back on my butt. Hillary's cabin buddies were searching for the bucket. I jumped up just in time to see Hillary bend over to grab the bucket with both hands from under a bunk.

"Here we go," I thought, "she's gonna have the last laugh."

Well, the next thing I knew, she jerked the bucket up and

hit her head on the top bunk. The force of the blow made her drop the bucket, so the water shot up into her face. Then Hillary fell backwards on her friend and they both went down in a heap. I had escaped the dreaded bucket of cold water!

I took off into the woods, never to be seen again by camp counselors. I lived off the land hunting rabbits with a slingshot, killing snakes with big sticks, and holding off bears with my trusty pocket knife.

In Cahoots

My dad was cool. He helped me out of two jams. The first was a ticket. As a teen, I had a lead foot driving around my little Volkswagen convertible. Some say my foot is still made of lead. I dispute that. But this day, I truly did. I was supposed to be doing 55 going around downtown Richmond, Virginia on Interstate 95. I was right there before the Broad Street exit when I got pulled over doing 86 in a 55. Well, in Virginia, that was and still is considered reckless driving. In Virginia, you can technically go to jail for that. But this cop just gave me a ticket like they usually do. The fine was some obscene amount of dough for keeping the state's coffers full of moolah. I could go to court. Pay the ticket and be done with it, or show that my speedometer was not working and pay no fine. So, my dad got an "adapter," shall we say. Maybe you could say a "device," a very special device that gets you out of a fine that's over 700 dollars.

Now, today I don't know if this could work. But back in the day, the "adapter" was the ticket out. Pun intended. Dad installed it then took me to an auto shop for a calibration report. When the mechanic checked my car, it was fine up to 35. After that, the guy indicated the speedometer would get to 35 and then it would start acting really weird. It threw all kinds of speeds at you—nothing regular. So, I took the report to court and got out of the speeding ticket.

The second time my dad helped me out of a jam was for Senior Skip Day. The morning of the big day I told him I really wanted to miss school because it was Skip Day for Seniors. He understood it was a special day for me and said

he would take care of it.

My dad's job was to maintain medical equipment.

That morning, he went to the hospital and was walking by a desk when he saw a doctor had left out his prescription ledger. So, my dad ripped off a note, forged a sick excuse, and signed it. I don't remember what the doctor's name was that he signed as, but you know, doctors have crappy script, so it didn't matter. Besides, it had the official letterhead with the doctor's info.

The next day, I found out 82% of my class skipped.

That was a record for Colonial Heights High School.

The building was a ghost town since kids in other class years skipped too. The next day and several days after that, the PA system called out the names of seniors, ordering them to the office to explain their reason for being absent. If you didn't have a valid excuse, like a doctor's note, you got demerits, which could lead to an ISS, in-school suspension. Well, when I got to Mr. Goulder's office, the vice principal, I was delighted I had the golden sick note.

Okay, it wasn't golden, but it sure felt like gold to me.

Mr. Goulder looked at it and said, "Nah, you forged this."

"What!" I said. "Can't you see that's an official doctor's letterhead? I was sick, Mr. Goulder."

He smirked and said, "Hmm, have a nice day, Trudi."

So I left with a gleeful smile on my face.

My mom, of course, found out what dad had done and told him that was lying. He ignored her. She was always fussing about something because my dad was always doing something he shouldn't be doing. So I dodged that bullet. My dad was and is so cool.

WORD PUZZLE

Directions: Throughout this book are hidden letters in the large illustrations. Place the letters in the correct order to spell the mystery words:

__ __ __ __ __   __ __ __ __ __ __ __

If you're stumped, the answer is on the next page.

Answer: Trudi Fruitie